The Truth

K SJ BOWLING

authorHOUSE®

AuthorHouse™ UK
1663 Liberty Drive
Bloomington, IN 47403   USA
www.authorhouse.co.uk
Phone: 0800 047 8203 (Domestic TFN)
        +44 1908 723714 (International)

Published by AuthorHouse 01/09/2020

ISBN: 978-1-7283-9524-1 (sc)
ISBN: 978-1-7283-9523-4 (e)

For Anna and the rest of my family:
those bonded
by blood and those by beer-
be they near or impossibly far

Thanks

Thank you to all those that have helped and supported
me in which ever way they were able, even when
unrecognised at the time. In any case
there are far too many to name
here and in honesty I think they would most likely
prefer to remain anonymous.

Anyway, my gratitude is truly endless
and hopefully I'll do them proud in the pages that follow
and in the years to come.

Contents

Foreword

This book is a collection of poems written by the author
over a span of the last 15 years. The first of which
being 'Wild Flowers' originally wrote in 2005.
Many of the poems featured here were written at turbulent
times including but are not limited to bereavement,
persistent self-doubts and problems with mental health
and you could say kind of serve as a diary of events.
Though it must be stated that the poems presented
here are not placed in any particular order according
to the dates in which they were originally written.

In addition to the above, any names of real persons
mentioned have been changed for the sake of anonymity.

So there's this girl

I know this girl
She's pretty cool
She dark and slim and not too tall:

She can draw
She can swim
She can write
She can sing

She can dance
She can run
She can listen and talk
She can ride a bike (and is totally self-taught)
She can laugh
She can cry
(A part of me thinks she may even be able to fly)

She can flirt
She can fuck
She can fight
She can duck
She's really brave and not short on luck
She can cook
She can throw
She continues to grow...

She has amused brown eyes
And a wicked sweet smile
On occasion she's been known to go a bit wild

Her name is Kadene and she's a fucking G!
You mess with her
You mess with me.

Wild Flowers

Wild flowers all grown tall of a scattered seed
Of a wild flower thrown far-
Too far for our eyes to see

One wild flower grew up and through cracks in the cement
Defiant, bold and often where the wise do fear to tread

Another flower was brought forth in a neglected field
With other wild flowers just the same, all warring for a
distant sun so more flowers they can yield

More wild flowers grew up wily and thin behind bike sheds
where kids do what they please
Determined to stay gripped to shallow roots as they thrash
about in this fierce breeze

Yet another flower grew out of dung under a grand oak tree
Tirelessly reaching for the light known to be there but still
yet to be seen

A wild flower climbs up on your lawn right now
Un-nurtured and still she grows
Until she too brings forth pollen and seed to be scattered to
the winds of which she has been sewn

The God That Warms

Watch the fire, son
That's your desire burning
Look into it deeper
You'll see all that you seek
Gaze into it forever just forever keep it from arms reach

Move a little closer to warm you against the closing night
Hold it in your fist for it's bright to negate the need for the
night-time's sight
Step into it's heart and be consumed by it whole
Feel it's warmth turn to heat and burn body, mind and soul

The Alchemist

Magic marks our meeting
Mountains could cross land and sea
Planets collide
Comets fly
Angels pull stars from heaven for just you and me

Between us a reaction is made
Kinetic and explosive and with it an undeniable change
...Even the big bang ain't got shit on us

We're both cellular and atomic
Intense and hotter than the Sun
Apart, you and I are cold
But babe, in you and me coming together
We can turn lead into solid gold

Natives and Serpents

Where does fortune follow?
The ceaseless unfolding tide
Cardboard ship and homemade compass
Wind blows fierce but on the captains side

Will I find land ahead with friendly natives baring flora and
fruit in open arms or an endless sea of snarling serpents with
froth at snaggled teeth, circling beneath
waiting to tear my water sodden ship apart?

Will the gods be kind and favour my direction or push me on
to Circe's isle of lotus fruit and wine?
My crew and I suspended in time like discarded marionettes and
the grand kinetic puppeteer finally gets his toilet break.

I must remember to sleep this close to the pole and wipe the
sleet from my eyes
Keep one hand on my compass; the other close to my heart
at all times

Freezing rain has drenched me through the sky ahead is
breaking
I marvel at a glimpse of the Sun behind oppressive clouds and
am shortly blinded by a beam that breaks through...

or was that lightning?

A Wet Day in Heaven

It's a wet day in heaven
The sun has not been seen
A gentle patter from warm grey clouds can be heard on all
the leaves
The sun, she rests behind the mist and will not be stirred
from sleep
She waits to rise another day when from joy the heavens cease
to weep
The fireflies do her work today as they dodge raindrops and
all those hungry beaks
Dragonflies skim the water and flirt, the frogs belch out
there beat
An owl shakes her feathers dry, does and stags all graze in
peace
And all else in heaven is still, it's silence long and sweet

The Rise

They thought me a mountain
Snow topped stoic and still
As unmoveable as the heavens and permanent as time himself

Little did they know the sleeping volcano
Red molten rock at my core
Churning and rising from deep down within
Racing for the brim
Waiting to spill forth my heated guts

Throwing charred confetti into the air in unbounded celebration
So all the world may marvel at my heart trembling power
(cower if you will, just don't miss the display)
A burning spirit freed and set flowing in slow streams and pools of a deep glowing sun

My immense heat
My deliberate steady currents
Born into lives of their own and unstoppable now
A permanent change to all it touches; blessed and scorched forever

Embers fly and bow in sudden modesty of their height
Crashing clumsy on the slow and those that dwell too close by-
A devastating and beautiful sight only the fearless can bare

(Though this is a mere future potential, a timeline to be strayed from or followed should I stay the course)

For now I doze under snowy sheets
The occasional burp of smoke escapes me
A fair warning to be prepared for anyone taking heed

Tall and still am I but no mountain stands here
Something warmer, more restless and reckless than the
patient cliffs and rolling hills holds their place

For I am a sleepy volcano stirring and some day all will rise
and run in the wake of my thunderous call

Survival in the Psyche ward

We're all political prisoners here
Each one a philosopher
Pondering patterns in time
Thrice daily meals
The birds
The weather
Television:
Our collective poison well, predictor of doubts, static alethiometer and black box beacon signal

They say a shaman learns to swim in the same waters a schizophrenic drowns and each one of us without a life preserver
Impatient in-patients cannot climb walls if there's nothing left to grip onto
Belts, sharps, sense and hippocratics left at the door
Every door is watertight and we try to imitate that gesture; lest these doctors learn the true depth of our thinking
The brutal bloody war between love and terror that hides in these unknown, caged hearts

Woman

They may sit in wonder on how it is I remain so strong.
And the answer is simple:

Because I am a woman

We rip ourselves in half to bring life into this world daily
We can bleed for days on end and may never be drained of life
We love without memory of its pain though we may carry
the scars:
this is a curse as well as a blessing
We are living breathing walking portals. Every. Single. One.
-A seamless link between the realm of spirit and this material
world lies between your legs

I am strong because I am powered from within
I am strong because I was weak for too long
I am strong because I have no choice
I am strong because I am woman.

F*cking Hippy

Be gentle with each other
Words and actions ripple across all existence

Love
Love
And love some more
If someone hates you
If someone hurts you
Fuck it, love 'em harder
They are those most in need of it

Ongoing Complaint of an Angry Black Woman

Forget the girl you see before you
Can you hear my voice
Close your eyes for just a moment and surrender to the dark
behind your lids
Your place of rest when given the choice

You've seen the shadow on cave walls now let you hear my verse
You may not like what I have to say but my silence would be
worst
This cave of shadows that is your living room holds a lie so
old it seems a slice of history we quietly all hold dear.
The black woman's bad bitch, her son a good shade worst; the
proof there for all to see
Stirred in with our sweet nostalgia
Those hazy good old days
How things of times passed never were but should have always
stayed

Black market, little white lie, blackmail, black as sin!
These are more than just a list of words but *fair* parallels to
the predicament that we all find ourselves in

The true colour of vanilla, the steady earth that holds us and
star dusted sky
Alas a beauty so long concealed is barely recognised
A crude caricature has its place with what seems increased
momentum of inequal balance to the volume of our growing
pride
Ignoring the mitochondrial, metaphorical mother of man:
The original human homo-sapien prototype; Darwin and Sir
Galton's inconvenient, unfortunate blind side

At the moment of each conception
Life starts with an explosion of that melanin
That very thing that plays with the light within my skin
That very thing so shunned and feared without which the
zygote that became you and anyone you've ever known would
have no start point with which to begin

We haven't even scratched the surface yet
They can not break this skin!
Make light of my complaints all you wish but a voice with no
face will always be mistaken for the wind

Long laughter at this invisible black girl trick do little but
to trivialise this life
Walking a mile in my running shoes would not nearly be
enough

You glimpse our horror and shrug, safe in the knowledge
that's no friend of yours; she must have done something; her
life must be set to a different sort of song
And anyway how could you possibly relate? She didn't have
your Gabby's hair *or* eyes. The nose was different. The colours
were all wrong

For Tomorrow we Work

Sleep now you strange child of the deep
For tomorrow our real work begins
We'll seek out the shallow water and rise up high
In effort to unite all far-flung kin
Close your eyes now and be at peace
That rare precious thing you're in search of is already set within
We'll bring it forth and show the world in effort to quiet this din

The God That Preserves

It's safe here in the dark, Mama
Do not fear for me
The cold, it keeps the devils at bay and here I cannot be seen
Here predators with the warm eyes of day won't think to search for me
It's cold here in the dark, Mama but here I can be free

Gears of Duty: Modern Halo

Artful illusionists are at play in our cities sands and trees
Suspended in air, invisible and thick like clear smoke,
choking all it reaches
Performing their grand acts of immortality
Validating there death defying feats with the mortal end of
each audience

From miles away children watch on in awe through thick
glass
Wool-wrapped and warm in artificial wombs, waving their
own magic wands
And patiently wait the day they too may boldly cheat death

Or be met half way

Scholars in skill yet to tread an oratory stage
A ten year old marksman: eager, ready and trained

Blank Paper

I've become so used to reading between the lines I think I've
ceased to see them

                          -to the untrained eye, a chaotic mess.

Knowing your position

                    on an unruled

                                                        page
isn't easy-
          you must be

                              heavy to hold

              your weight.

Press hard and be steady to

                                    make your mark,

your self-governed hand

                    alone

                              must keep you

              straight.

Green Eggs and Ham

Eating generational curses for breakfast ain't easy
It's a tough course to digest
The taste is vile and nobody wants to touch it, you have to
eat your whole families portion even that of those long dead.
Like eating the greens your mother's own child like hands
wouldn't touch-
The nutrition she spat out- now sits still waiting for you at
the dinner table but with years of rot, and her mother's and
hers and hers...

You could leave it all but someone has to eat it.
Can you really wait for your children to clear the plate?

All men are beasts but for a blessed few
That can take all of their rage and fear and melancholy,
The fuel that feeds the thing that feasts upon them;
And temper it into something strong, beautiful and worthy
of awe.

A talisman against past demons. A souvenir of suffering
overcome.
And in doing so they become something akin to a god or an
angel within themselves in this human form

(A Conversation between:) The Microbiologist and the Astrophysicist

The Microbiologist

At my desk last night looking at samples a colleague left with me, hunched over my microscope- what do you think I saw? Nothing less than a little man staring back at me. I adjusted the lense to get a closer look and he must have done the same, he scribbled something down then held up a sign that asked me of my name. I answered back the little man the best I could guess how. With haste and excitement he scribbled down "oh shit, that's my name too!" the best I could think to say was "wow".

He asked me how this was possible but his guess was as good as mine! I asked him what he was searching for and what he hoped to find. He told me that his world was vast but he had found few answers there. He hoped to glimpse at other worlds and prove to himself that there was little to fear.

He asked me of me my aims and I told him I sought the secrets to life, he said our lives' work had much in common and maybe we should both call it a night! This microscopic man, so small and droll, gave understanding to holes in my research I could never hope to find, a universe lies within every cell? The thought itself was more than enough to blow the broadest mind.

He told me the names of constellations and star clusters, one just to my right. I dared not tell him that one was actually a colleague I despise. In spite I feigned my ignorance and didn't give his name but this homunculus man deserved to know to my enduring shame. We talked on at length on all and nothing; he asked if aliens were real- I had my doubts and he had none, his passion on which was tangible enough to feel. I asked him how many more men like him there were, he answered several million and a million more then listed off another dozen common species he thought I'd never heard of before.

He said he was a lonely man as our conversation continued to unfurl, I almost wept for him and all the lonely millions in my own world. He asked me about blackholes and the possibility of time travel around distant dark suns and shared the pensive, flattering notion that anti matter was merely oxygen circulating my lungs! He actually asked if I was God, I told him no with honesty and as the sun rose those very words came full circle, returning back to me. I watched it rise and wondered on the true nature of all my eyes can see, was this sun just a ball of wild gases or another greater star-man's eyes gazing down at me?

We agreed to speak the following night but on my return he had put his telescope away. He shuffled bent, slower than before and all his hair had turned grey. I did try to speak as I did before but he could not hear me. The following night he was gone altogether, his tower curiously dark and free of eyes that seek.

The Astrophysicist

In my gazing tower, looking through my telescope you'd never guess what it was I'd seen: The giant eye of a giant man staring down at me. At first I thought him stardust or a group of distant galaxies, but then he blinked and I was sure- as implausible as it seemed! I took a sheet and noted down in

21

the largest hand I could "what's your name?" A short time on a voice answered in both a whisper and a boom.

"It's G" he said, which damn near bowled me over for that is my name too. I had to sit down for just a moment and question all I felt I knew. He pointed a little way off and commented on the beauty of our streets- he called it bioluminescence, I called them street-lamps, his laughter at which vibrated right through me. He asked many questions and I the same, and we both answered the best we could. I felt more a priest speaking with himself or his god by the end than any scientist should! He asked me of a changing mass just a few feet away from me, remembering my surrounding I looked around but it was something I could not see. I told him this and the man's surprise was just as great as mine- at the very notion that at such distance his eyes could see that which mine could never find.

I told this star-mass man of my research and my knowledge of all the alien suns, as I spoke I wondered if I was really speaking of this man's left ear or the chewed down nail of a thumb. He told me of his family, his wife and new born twin sons, which lead to a lengthy discussion as to whether the universes numbered more than one.

He asked me of my hobbies and what I did for fun, I had to tell him that work was my life and life my work and my hobbies next to none. To change the subject I asked what he knew of wormholes and blackholes and mysteries of the like, he correctly stated the blackholes were really suns so heavy that their gravities clutched tight to even time and light. He asked what I felt distant planets held and after some thought I answered "much the same" and as I did the sky filled with clouds and it began to rain.

He told me his sun was rising and it was time for him to get some sleep. This boggled my mind even further, I'm not afraid to say that from my joy I did nearly weep. Before he went, I had to ask if he was god and the meaning to life; "to be happy, I guess." Was all he said- a fair and honest reply.

We agreed to speak the following night but he never returned, much to my dismay. My research continues as does my hope that I'll speak with him again. I'll cast these eyes up every night but my fear remains the same, that never more will those starry eyes be set to cast this way.

Storm Under the sky

Earth is prison riot:
Someone's written over the south wall in blue
Bloody handprints cover all the pillars
Men fall to their knees and pray for their mothers and home
A fire is burning somewhere; I can smell the smoke
But no-one seems to care
Those death row men are running wild, flipping all the switches
All I see are exit signs written up in green
Purple-blue electric dances on the ceiling and steals away to the upper levels
I hold my breath as the lights go out
I think there might be a storm

Your Untitled Mask

Is yours a face I should trust, love or despise?
What flows with my name as tumbles from your mouth in
my absence?

I want to trust you, I really do but that weathervane refuses
to pick a direction. I tell myself to trust in my wings so I may
never need confidence in your branches, be they sturdy or not.
But these wings...

My flapping arms exhausted

It would be nice to find a strong limb free from rot
Skip one night's flight at least
But these wings have been clipped so many times I still flinch
at your approach scissors in hand

You say it's to cut a heart from the red square of card you
keep tucked in your left breast pocket. You'll give it to me
when you're done.

But all I ever heard was "It's to cut a heart"

Now I'm all for the Timotei effect, flicking water from hair in an arch of perfect spray;

Emerging from a sparkling spring. Exotic nubile young women with dark eyes, soft supple caramels thighs. But if you love the "exotic" love it as a whole- the way my hair stands firm; defiant even in strong breeze

How skin this soft cannot only take kisses but a full on make-out session with the Sun

How to be built big beautiful, love and know this and still be able to leg it for the number 2 bus!

To remain kind and caring and fantastically complex within when the world persistently tells you you are not!

To keep strong and continue pushing forward even when the mountains you move don't know that they can or simply refuse to budge.

That is a marvel to behold and true miracle

A rare strange beauty so seldom seen

Like an orchid growing wild down the highstreet in Peckham, the definition of exotic in its concentrated extreme.

The Gas Lamp

The gas lamp in my kitchen burned low yesterday
Mother sighed and said it had always been that way

The morning before the light shone bright with a high
leaping flame
Father laughed and swore it was exactly the same

That very evening it had dimmed again; I told my sister in
dismay
She looked at me with amusement and mischief and asked if
I was feeling okay

I lay abed for nights on end and wondered what was wrong
with my eyes
If I had gone mad
If I was going blind
All the time I could hear scratches and clinks
Tinkering from the kitchen below
I thought to investigate but my fear had laid me low

This morning the lamp was so low it barely held its flame
But the light
Was as steady as ever, or so my big brother claimed

My friends all chimed in agreement saying the gas lamp's
light is strong-
My mouth said "you're right, of course!"
My heart knew that was wrong

Art

Life laid out for a silent church mouse
Marigolds glued at the sleeves
No need for knowledge, experience
Nor comradery
No need for shoes: you'll never leave

Then came that call at a catalytic age
Too shy to walk by light of day
I hid in the comfort of night's shadow instead

On a wander one night I met a man at midnight
Standing at a lonely crossroad, gleaming
He took my hand and held it tight, whispered "do or die"
With a smile glinting brilliant in snow white

He took my eyes and gave me his
They burnt me and the whole world through, right down to
the bones

Galvanized by my new burning sight I ran headlong and deep
into darkness
Without a glance back;
Shredding naïve soft skin on the souls of my feet with barely
a flinch or care
These eyes know what benefits only broken beer bottles can
bring

Breath lost on bridge
I met a company of two, at three
A beautiful pair of strangers stood waiting
A man named Music and his daughter named Dance-
He welcomed me with tears and kissed my scorched eyes

She greeted me with a smile and embrace as warm as Summer

Music was deaf and his daughter mute;
The language between them clear and strange
Music stole the voice of God to make it his own
But was deafened by his own first uttered words
Though heart wrenching and rhythmic; sweet, fearsome and low-
Music's own voice he'd never known

Dance moved with unfathomable grace and a way of looking at you
That displayed every thought and dream in her soft glowing soul
And bliss lay there still in her sweet silence, content without verse
Confident to speak with clarity and freedom outside the clumsy world of words

Together they bound my feet to stop the swell
Clothed and fed and wished me well
They did not cling but pushed me forth into a world I thought myself not ready for

As dawn broke I passed a dog called Science, too busy chasing his tail
Desperate to examine his furthest ends in the finest detail
I wagged a ragged branch before his eyes and flung it further than I could see
You should have seen the smile on his sandy face as he ran to pursue-
I look of surprise, wonder and glee

The Sun hung high and beat down hard
And I walked proud
No longer afraid to be seen

I reached a lake and stripped to the skin-
Took no hesitation to dive right in
I swam on my back from shore to shore
Gazing at a broad lilac sky
Pondering my journey and life itself- questioning who I am
and why
Then lightening struck my watery bed and rippled across,
carrying the answer to me:

"I am Art" I proclaimed aloud, "for now and eternity"

Dreams Bond

All aboard the Dream Boat!
We're about to leave shore
A cruise ship sets sail for nirvana
Busy, restless and unsure

But there's an enigmatic stranger on top deck
A Cupid pistol strapped at his waist
I see him atop a flight of stairs and the auto-navigator sets
to pursue
But the crowds are thick and vast and I loose him
Never seeing his face

Now I'm on top deck with him
It's not night anymore!
The sea is beaten blue and Sun bright
But how did we get here?

This bugs me for a while

We're at a summer training camp:
He makes giant balls from rubber bands and I do boxing
Holding my own against rough female antagonists

I doze in a dormitory for boys and girls but I'm the only one
sleeping-
He softly scratches at my hand to wake me up and asks me to
meet him in the cellar
But I hang back, saying morning to my fellow trainees and
take a little too long

By the time I reach the heavy water tight doors, I'm just in time to watch him climb the paint-peeled rusting steps again and off to his bed

I'm in my ex-beau's house but he's not there and I'm waiting for *him*
It's getting light; he's not going to make it so I prepare to leave, turning off the bathroom light
But still I wait anyway...

Then he's there!
We share a beanbag and talk close with a whiskey and coke and a DS mini; coloured lights on a display
He rests a hand half way up between my thighs but my skirt is tight and taught and will move no further

I giggle a happy secret

It's Christmas Eve
I see faces from childhood and years long passed
Spies and saboteurs laugh languidly
I spot him across a crowded room and a silent prayer beckons him over but my defences are up when we exchange few words
I feel eyes watching...

But wait!

Did he just say he loves me?
Or am I still dreaming?

Just a Thought

It is (im)possible to attract more luck than you are given?
Luck has a will, spirit and desire all it's own; some would call her Serendipity.

She may choose to cling to one throughout life like the static charged dust on a TV screen, or to desert a new born life before it's even had chance to draw it's first breath (or maybe its us missing a trick, we drudging through whilst they sit this round out?)

For some luck is like a childhood friend; ever present in the early years, then drifts and fades to be nothing more than a memory. Luckily, for most she's more like a casual acquaintance; dipping in and out periodically through life brightening it up whenever she appears even if only for a few moments.

Maybe luck is no more than the positive outcome of chance and if so, the only way to truly increase your luck is to increase your chances taken. Though doing this swings a double edge sword as with all chance comes risk and an increase in chances taken is also an increase in risk and all round failure.

So the question remains, what would you prefer: To live out life with your raffle drawn luck, or risk all your given chances for death or glory?

In short, or so I'm told-
"Be bold, and grand forces will come to your aid."

Children of Adam

Adam and Eve were fire breathers. Darker than jet. Both had three eyes and stood taller than any silicon. That all changed the day they ate of the fruit from that tree. One taste made them think they knew all, to see better they closed one eye and made themselves shrink small. They walked out and away from Eden and grew paler with every step and found themselves crude shelter when the need came to rest. To survive they learned to drink of each other's blood and set about to explore this new brave world. They bore many sons and daughters and in time they bore their own and one day their great grandchildren would return to Eden to collect what they felt they owned. They'd return with iron and crosses. They'd return with armoured men. Eden's children will still be three-eyed fire breathers but what would they be then?

The day the Sun Held its Breath

The day the sun held its breath was your average Saturday. She was beating down in some places and in others, they had their rain.

But way off out in space, the sun was in a tiz about changes in her neighbourhood and the state all things were in. She held her breath for just a moment to clear her thoughts and all the solar system halted in it's spin.

In some places the sun did not set that day and in others it didn't rise. And all trees and flowers alike began to wilt much to the worry of the wise.

This world herself stopped for just a moment and all within her held their breath, to see if this was the catalyst to life's beginning or the beginning of all life's death.

But the world she kept on ticking as she always has done best, as she no need for pause and not a cause for rest.

The sun let out a sigh eventually and all caught up in its time, though she had hoped to answer questions that unfortunately still alluded her already busy mind.

Earth barely seemed to notice, though many had begun to pray and vowed to keep their sun stress free and breathing to rise another day.

A Clockwork to it

And how can you not be humbled in the face of the universe
at work
When all things come together to show you and know
There is a clockwork to it
Something to connect all things
Every atom then becomes a cog
What space between them, spring
The smallest action has its gravitas and grandeur
And hearts heavy can pull all into their orbit to become one
with their every beat and swing

Then even you could be surprised to find that your name's
been written across the stars
Whispered through the centuries to find it's way to your
mother's ears
Our names are in opus somewhere, scripted it ancient tome
Detailing deeds far into distant futures to even the writer's
hands unknown

All things flowing and eternal
Yet not all set in stone
Like all waters cannot help but flow to the sea
All paths carved to a single kismet to only our deepest
conscious known

Incarnation of a Khaleesi

You want my death to be easy for you

To take the rope to my neck
A blade to my wrist
A quick plunge through cold air...

Well tough.

I am not that kind
I am not so obedient
I will not go gently
I will make a scene
You will have to kill me
And yes! It will be messy

I'll fight you to the final breath

I will not cut this journey short just to please you-
Just to suit your whim and need

But with hope and if nothing else this will demonstrate the
force of my will
Testament to the bigger beasts met that had no option but to
leave me standing
Of how a woman the likes of me can bathe in fire and not
burn

This too Shall Pass

Whatever it is your going through
However little you think the others would understand
Whoever's put you to trial and test
Be brave even when there's no one there to lend or take your hand
Just know that this too shall pass; the sun shall rise to catch up with the dawn

To come forth by day is a beautiful thing, the dark shall set and all known things will be glad to greet another morn
Live to fight and love and laugh another day when justice is reborn
This too shall pass
This too shall pass
Believe this word and keep it safe to whisper as and when you need
Remember all things have their season and yours my friend may well be here far sooner than it has ever been

Wicked Men

Modern man needs one good slap!
To set him back in place
Steer him back on track
So far has he strayed from civility grace and tact-
The gentleman died of old age is the sad and cold fact.

Minds washed down to one basic idea: housemaid or pornstar,
the choice is made clear
Reserved courtesy for their Sunday night best; covered puddle
pour vous, choke on this dick and cock in the arse for the rest.

No-one warned me of this dark nature in men to which a
child's mind is blind
Mother hid my eyes
Showed me agreed upon lies
Of head strong princesses and gallant princes
Maidens in towers with impossibly long hair
And I gobbled them whole!
My youthful heart eager to believe this future feasible and
waiting for us all.
And when doubt crept in I fought back
Shouting with fingers in ears stubborn to believe these were
the true facts

Beloved brothers, as if children
Mother's love like a bed of hot coals
Father wanders grieving a lost childhood
So over time and alone I would embrace all I have come to
know

Through my gender's legacy
My eve gene at its play
A task's been assigned
Baring painstakingly forged armor of beautiful flesh and
bone
Each carved in our own magnificent design.

But what of the rest?

Teenage girls catching money you throw in thongs or less,
saying you'd split her in half without the faintest scent of
irony in your words.
Or the amateur professionals the right side of the bar, lacking
their plates of mineral hardened through Their patient
optimism only serving as a cruel corrosive device
Keeping their tender forming amour brittle and thin and
pride alone keeping them steady in stride

They are eagerly pierced through the chest time and again by
killers bearing kind smiles

And now their captor hold a new toy for the same old game
Forsaking all known bounds for the sake of its name:
Visioning dirty magicians
Blooming Bella Donnas
Or searing angels with no wings

Instead of someone's sister
A long lost childhood friend
A once cherished and forgotten nervous first lover
Or god forbid another human being

But then that generous and charming devil releases his
bewildered prey and here the witch-hunt can begin:

Aim a dart filled with all shades of off-loaded guilt and
blame squarely at the back of her head as she flees to lick her
poisoned wounds.
The only evidence of any event being demonizing tales of
woman leading man astray and scars she'll never show you
Just ask Delilah and Eve, they know the drill

And tomorrow he'll be free to do it all again, with a skip in
his step and a pillaged smile on his face- making certain to
utilize the full essence of his catch
I hold no blade but my armor is sturdy and tough and shines
so bright the blind find it hard to ignore. All the filth and
gore will wash right off with a just little love and courageous
might.

                              Hands up who's feeling brave

But what of the rest?

The ones pushed into the ground
So far down
No shield to protect from the crushing weight
Broken feet and no nails left to manicure from trying to claw
themselves out

From half the world over
Behind unassuming doors down quaint suburban streets
In attics bedrooms basements cupboards- too easily turned
coffins

Waiting in dread or numbness to be filled out with promise
of working off some unknown debt
No time limit and no interest, guaranteed

Someone needs to stand up
Nah, more than one.

Not out of friendship or love but for human dignity
Integrity
And because that's what our hearts would tell us is right
If we'd only allow ourselves to hear it

But in all my years it's just a handful of hopefuls
Like pigmy Amazonians
Waiting with war paint on ready for a hero's fight
And yes those same marred warriors of Boudicca's brave seven
daughters
Set drifting in a sea of armies of one
Pulled along with the confused and angry tide

So bare in mind whilst your off professing gallantry and
valor to your own ends
Chaos with liquor in clubhouses for boys
Made from the ruins of your grandfather's tomb-like tool shed
To you I ask and please don't laugh:

Who can your sisters
Mothers
Children, ever truly trust
To help protect us
From these wicked men?

The Woman Eater

They're coming for us, I can feel it
Take a good long now because I am of a dying breed
Soon there will be none of us left
Just a whispered half memory

Women of intelligence, kind heart and passionate opinion
with beauty and substance Far surpassing what the eye sees
will be obliterated from your lives,
Our futures
Our histories

They'll reduce us to nothing more than titillating mutes for
carnal use-
Oil paintings with glory holes (turn your TV on a while to
check for signs of proof)
Many moons ago it seems we were handed the illusion of
equality
And we were so grateful after centuries of dwindling patience
we never thought to look our Trojan gift horse in the mouth

Now forward 40 years or more to when the gift reveal its curse:
As we screamed "Girl Power!" in red lipstick and mini-skirts,
all smiles and peace signs: they seized their chance to creep
in, reattached the chains, told us what good brave girls we
all were, patted us on the knee and once again locked us in

It maybe their doctrine but its our desire to be desired that
pumps blood through the veins of this female famished beast

And with that
We signed our own death certificate
Extinction it seems is now imminent

They say women claim they no longer need feminism
These women are wrong and not just them-
Just remember if you think this doesn't apply:
First they'll come for the women
Then they'll take the men.

Bruja

The condemned witch stood before them
A sharp breeze at her skirts and heels
A vast storm cloud hung just above her
Hands bound to protect the crowd from her demonic skills

She stepped forward and bowed her head then for her twined
necklace raised it high. They stood arm to arm all sides of
her with crucifix, axe and scythe.
The priest bravely moved closer and asked her if she had
anything left to add or if she wished for them to pray
She entranced him aside and cleared her throat, entrusted
her voice to the wind to say:

"All you that stand before me, know this here and now; from
this day now know that none of you stand free, anyone of you
could be stood here in place of me
You there Mr Baker, I've seen you weep and plead to the
crescent moon that she might release you from the pain of
knowing what your wife does with our young Deacon Boone
Or you there Mrs Waldon, don't look at me that way- I saw you
watching us dancing in the moonlit fields, your expression
was far from that of dismay

One of your brood among us, you know which one; she told me
how the two of you reminisced on the mischief of your heyday
And you butcher Pete, I saw you spy me in the long grass as I
swam naked in the swollen stream, you lingered a little long for
someone mere concerned to me at least it seems
And you tailor John, you were with him. Where's your sweet
wife tonight? She came to me not two moons passed saying
she feared for her life

She told me as we bound her wounds he gave her fresh that day 'If I'm gone don't leave the kids with him' the last I heard her say
"You only told on me before I could tell on you. There's a place up here for all of you!
Maybe I laughed to loudly
Maybe my words were too curt
Too opinionated for a woman unmarried and unmoved back that or lack of wealth. Lay with too many of your husbands though you all do that enough amongst yourselves
Forgot my bonnet to the country faire one too many times, helped you with issues of fertility, fever or poor rest
Taught your daughters to read and write in secret before their masters and fathers could sell them on and teach them to be less."

A clamour rose throughout the crowd. She raised her eyes to the heavens for help
and was met with a whip of light and wild cracking sound
She said something into the din but no one heard, she breathed deep to bellow loud:

"I curse you all! Hear me and soon see, from this day forth with naught but daughters with blazing hearts and minds the likes of me
May the righteous of this parish be blessed with the same plus enough sons for you all.
Don't look for them here among you now, they want no part in this spectacle
May my name be their first words, though you'll cease to speak of me from this the first of your damned days!
Rise up over you dishonourable forefathers and drive all your ilk away."

She spat at the ground but the wind picked it up and flung it in the hangman's face, she raised her eyes to the sky one last time and laughed long and loud as a tear finally cleared one cheek

But soon her laughter turned to a scream; the crowd winced from her sorcery.

"Gods please send me a looking glass so I may show all of these your children what it is I see

I swear I never lay with their unholy god! I know my soul is priceless and can't be sold for even the highest fee

I confess I lay with Jack son of Joe, Mr Baker and Mrs Greenleaf, and Lord Marston when summoned to his halls or when sent to his priest

Though the last of these trespasses was not of my choice- I beaten and bought to him in bonds, forbade to use my voice

And it would have been my sweet sister if not me; Sacred Mother protect her please

Forgive me for all wrongs I've done and for—" The priest had had and heard enough the hangman's job now done

She flew for just a moment, folk said she meant to fly away. Before god's tether caught and held her and there she stayed and swayed

A low rumbled was heard in the distance

The storm was moving away

An ill fit hush held over the square even after the town went on to carry out the rest of its day

The tailor's wife never was seen again- their eldest taken her place as mother, wife and meat

The stream swelled again but burst its banks and drowned out half the corn and wheat

Not a single boy was born the following year though all girls
were healthy and happy with ten fingers on chubby hands and
ten toes on chubby feet
And no one ever did mention her name again, just held their
collective breath and waited for their daughters to speak.

That Distant Lime Green Light

I sent my heart ahead to meet me in heaven-
I hope it knows the way
For upon my death I'll use its light as a beacon
so I may move forth without delay

This land, it made her sick and she wasted
Trapped tight in this stifling rib cage
And in freeing her I freed myself-
Our debts to each other now triple paid

This body strong but soul was dying with parts that had no
wish to stay
We both have what we need for this here present and set to
re-unite on that distant day

No Breeder of Chaos

Light can be found in the darkness
If you don't believe me just look at the night's sky
And the light, it holds many a dark thought
Stare into the flame and you'll see for yourself why

I am no breeder of chaos
Just a girl seeking to open my eyes
To stir from this waking coma, stretch and be free from these
stubborn lies

The Abyss

I found strength in my vulnerability
The beauty in these ugly scars
Found perfection in my failings
In the darkest ocean, a route to Mars

Public Service Announcement

Kill your television
There's little left for you there
Salvage what hasn't been taken yet, make for high ground
And take the high road there

Take a guitar, a few good books, whatever pencils and paper
spare
Bring hammer and needle and thread
And your singing voice if you dare!

The glowing fourth wall of your front rooms been a fine old
friend
But screw it
Smash it good to break the hex!
Film the fray on your iPhone 23 and tell the phone it's next

All the Angels and Every Demon

I've come to realise the Gods exists
All the angels and every demon

They dwell within us
Beside us
Shifting shape and form
Roaming through
To fill and embrace whoever invites them in

And feed or feast on as much as you will allow them
Like every gracious guest

We see them with others and remain so sure we stand alone
Only recognising old friends* from afar

Our tragic folly is to reflect
To project
What the heart holds onto the nearest vessel
Too see our likeness at a distance and fail to see our own
mirrored form

Invictarius

And yes, we of our still diminishing republic shall take our
pride to the last
We shall not sway
We will stand strong
We will not go gentle into that good night
We may die where we stand and smile in the face of death
when he comes

For we are one woman
One form
One universe
May we never again be meek for that will surely mean our
doom

They can laugh at us and beat us but that can only touch the
skin
We are woman and stronger for it
We need not let them in

The Girl in the Stripy top

(I can't find my top)

[Act 1]

There's a girl in a stripy top on TV.
She's talking about comparing prices on the internet and tells
me not to do that to myself, she looks pretty business savvy
though so I guess she knows what she's talking about.
The girl in the stripy top is back again: This time she's about
fourteen, she has big round headphones on and looks annoyed.
Suspicious or intruded upon; insulted that her brother would
sneak up on her for such a photo opportunity. (Where'd I even
put that stripy top anyway?)
Now children are telling a man called Iain to talk to a girl:
It's her again!
She looks young and happy this time (I know an Iain, is that
weird? I wonder how he's been doing.)
She's in a light airy room now, bright green and stone grey,
She's a red head this time, setting the table for... dinner
maybe? (I don't know) Her husband's saying something about
her favourite food. "You won't tell her, will you?" he winks
right at me.

[Act 2]

Now she stands on a step ladder level to the kitchen table.
Skin: caramel and smooth. Hair: glossy yet wild and perfectly
coiled. Smiling wide; eyes on phone, phone in hand. (Oh look
at that, I have those dungarees too!)

[Act 3]

"Stop" She yells
And for a moment everything does
"This" she points in all directions "Is no game."
"This" she stamps one tiny tired foot "Is no spectator sport."
The girl in the stripy top screams until she turns an impossible
red. Throws a spatula across the room. Teeth clenched. Fists
tight enough to bleed, thrust high enough to let the blood
show.
She jumps down from the step ladder, clears the table of it's
spread, cuts the invisible rope and all the strings and throws
that damn phone straight at the camera man's head... then
come back to kick the camera over and sets it on fire!

The voiceover knows her lines: "The new lifestyle everyone
can enjoy." -But now she's stumped. "Do I carry on?" she says
to someone behind her- no audible answer...
The girl in the stripy top has climbed over the sink and out
the kitchen window, running for her own life over Astroturf
and through neat hedges. Shouting something about shadows
and caves and dreams and laughing like a woman crazed
under the full moon until no-one can see her and only the
echo of her happiness remains.
A silent cheer for her escapes the crease in my mouth. Did
they see it?

The TV seems to stutter, almost clears its throat
The screen goes blank for just a second then a grey cat springs
up to sell me food. He's trying to coax his prey from its hiding
place: this... majestic cat, full of flattery and charm is poised
and waiting "where are your eyes?" he asks.

I say "right here."

L

Lillith's in the first wives club!
She knows how it feels to be left behind
Omitted from the first chapter of the good book for not being
the blushing bride
It seems she was a little too outspoken
Maybe she put her own needs first
Didn't jump at Adams clicked fingers when time came she
was meant to give birth!
So Adam up and left her- found himself a paler bride
No-one knows what really happened to her with no courts or
alimony to decide
Maybe she found Caine and they wandered together
Or else she was Abel in another tongue
Like I say nobody knows; she probably just had to run

Light and Nature

Nobody, not one, can help these tricks of light and nature thrust upon us

Maybe the bees are black and yellow to both calm and excite the flower
Maybe the center of a flower in yellow to excite the bee

Red is the colour of creativity, sex and danger in the back of all minds; maybe because of the life force blood that runs through our veins:
It scares us when we see it but it's better to know it's there
Maybe it's that what links our need for violence against ourselves and others- to see the red and remind us that we indeed still live
And not to be gross but we women get that monthly reminder; and speaking of which is that not the natural indicator that we are ready to create life within ourselves?

Am I making any sense?

We fear the dark as children but is that not what you see when the time comes to sleep and close your eyes? Just as a flower does its growth in darkness, we need it just as much as we need the light

The lightning strike and its accompanied thunder scare many too but then why do we associate it with ideas?

And the water that replenishes us could drown us, a rational point of many fears, linked in mind to loyalty and emotion, the thing we release from our eyes when overwhelmed by the way of tears

Green is associated with both growth and eventual decay; we recognise more shades of this than any other and bring to mind life's eternal cycle and its full array

Everything has a purpose, even colour, or else we'd have the sight of dogs
And maybe dogs too lack our sight for a reason, if nothing else to make them brave and to go forth strong

Follow the Flame

A child of fire am I and that I shall remain
Raised by a red smoking hill I wandered far to find myself lost
Walking in woods late one day.

A tiger found me first with hunger in wild eyes, so savage
I was wise to run away.

Deep in the green a serpent slinked up to me and raised his head to say:
"Hey fire child, I know your people. What brings you out this way? It's getting dark- you best be gone, that brazen glow makes you easy prey. Come with me, fire girl I'll cover you with leaves; there is no need to stay. I'll keep you safe, we'll find your home, don't go seeking death today."
He seemed friendly enough and willing to help but against the waking stars my red mountain loomed.

Blinking torches a thousand miles off, an impossible lifetime away
Showed me where I should be and the road I must take, my course sure and clear, though no doubt I would make mistakes.
I gauged my surroundings to go ahead, said

"That's okay" to my viperant friend, "I can guess the way. Don't worry about me and thanks all the same, I'll just follow the flame."

As the last of light fled, a bear rose from his cave and beckoned I follow;
He seemed pretty tame.

I shook my head and walked on straight "No thanks babe, I'll just follow the flame."

Then the next to happen a red foxes call claimed to know the way.
"That's okay" I echoed right back "I'll just follow the flame."

In the thick of night with a buzz a bee offered his assistance but all I could think to say: That's okay honey, I've got this down. I'm just gonna follow the flame."

The nymph's song so sweet, I tried to repeat. It damn near led me astray.
They danced and danced of the edge of a cliff then giggled & fluttered away.
I had to shrugged and laughed it off "No worries sweetie and bon voyage! I'll just follow the flame."

At dawn a sweet wee doe bounded up and nuzzled one knee
At the foot of my hot mountain path she pleaded with me
"That's not your home" she pointed, eyes wet with dismay. "Stay close to me and I'll show you the way." Then with all good intent she trotted back just the way I came.

I smiled at her "That's quite alright, I'll just follow the flame."

Dream Fodder

A thousand rebel artist-angels gave me a piece of their heart
to patch the one I'd lost

Turned this girl back to the living and with a map drawn
with
their two thousand hands led her out of the land of ghosts

With eyes that quenged and saw through dreams and
nightmares
far further than any could possibly hope or ever dare

The well for fodder of life and dreams had always known
where to be
and how to meet her there

Fresh Water

Cast back your poisoned doubts to the waters in which you found them
Be not blind to your own good acts and deeds
Be rooted in the rich soil and cleansed in the water of fresh seas
Fire is all around you, you need not wear it on your sleeves

The Truth

If you really want to hurt someone
tell them the truth

If you want to make them angry
tell them the truth

Want to scare the shit out of them?
tell them the truth

If you want to set them free
Tell them the truth.

About the Author

K SJ Bowling was born in 1985 in South London, the city where she currently lives. She has studied Illustration, 16 mm Filmmaking and Creative Writing at various institutions across the city and has been writing poetry and short stories since the age of 14. This is her first book.

Lightning Source UK Ltd.
Milton Keynes UK
UKHW010753230320
360715UK00001B/9